Bear Grylls

SURVIVAL SKILLS HANDBOOK

FIRST AID

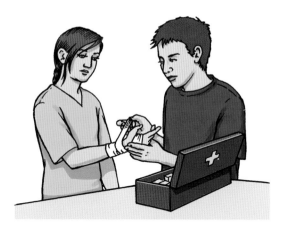

Bear Grylls

This survival skills handbook has been specially put together to help young explorers just like you to stay safe in the wild, and to be able to cope when things go wrong. There is always a risk of accidents happening in the wild, and it's important to know how to act in an emergency. This book will show you how to deal with the most common first aid situations, (although it's a good idea to go on a first aid training course too). Good knowledge, regularly practiced saves lives. I have seen this first hand many times.

Bear.

CONTENTS

INTRODUCTION TO FIRST AID

Unfortunately it is very common for people to become unwell or get involved in an accident. If you are keen to go outdoors and explore, it is important to understand some basic first aid. You should make sure an adult is nearby or knows your location at all times, but these handy tips can help keep you safe.

Getting training

If an accident occurs, somebody needs to take charge and decide what to do. You will feel safer and more confident if at least one person in your group has had some first aid training. There are lots of courses available in most towns, and these are often extremely enjoyable as well as teaching a really important life skill.

first aid kit

volunteer first aider

After training

You may decide that a simple understanding of first aid is enough for you, or you may find that you want to carry on learning after the basics and join a first aid organisiation.

First aid kit

It is useful to have at least a basic first aid kit for any outdoor situation. You will need to decide what to bring according to the acitvities you are planning, the time of year, the length of time you are out, and the needs of the people going with you.

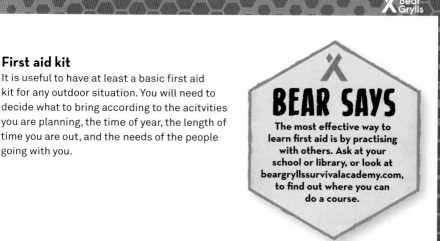

BEAR SAYS

The most effective way to learn first aid is by practising with others. Ask at your school or library, or look at beargryllssurvivalacademy.com, to find out where you can do a course.

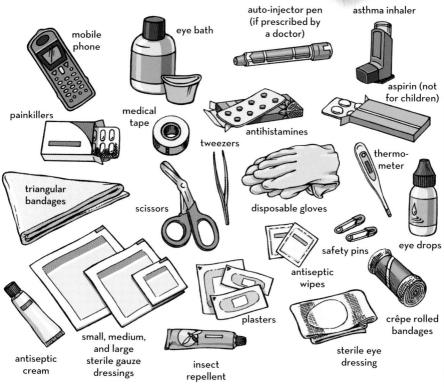

mobile phone

eye bath

auto-injector pen (if prescribed by a doctor)

asthma inhaler

painkillers

medical tape

antihistamines

aspirin (not for children)

tweezers

thermo-meter

triangular bandages

scissors

disposable gloves

eye drops

safety pins

antiseptic wipes

crêpe rolled bandages

antiseptic cream

small, medium, and large sterile gauze dressings

plasters

insect repellent

sterile eye dressing

PREVENTION

If you are planning a trip, it is very important to make a first aid plan so that everyone is clear what to do if there is a problem. If there are any doubts, it is best to postpone the trip until you feel confident that you can deal with any issues.

Preparation

Preventing first aid situations is far better than dealing with them. Make sure you wear the right footwear and take clothing appropriate for the weather conditions. Bring enough food and water for the time you will be out, and carry a mobile phone in order to call for help if you need it. Make sure you plan your route carefully, and that someone at home knows where you are going and when you expect to return.

Signs of life

It's often quite tricky to tell how serious a situation may be. Doctors spend years training and still sometimes find it difficult, so always call for help – it's better to be overly cautious than delay vital emergency services if someone is hurt.

- Shout loudly if they are unconscious. Use their name and ask if they can hear you.
- Gently shake their shoulders; If they are actually asleep this should wake them up.
- Tell the injured person you are about to call an ambulance if they are conscious.
- If someone else is with you, ask them to call the ambulance. Get them to tell you when they have done it or, if possible, do it near you.
- Check if the injured person is breathing. Their chest should go up and down. If you hold a mirror or metal spoon under their nose, their breath will steam it up. Wait at least 10 seconds.
- Check for a pulse on their wrist or the side of their neck – this is tricky and you really need to know what you are looking for. Try practising on yourself.

How to get help

You cannot help someone else if you put yourself in danger. It is important to check that the situation is safe for you and the injured person. If you can safely take steps to make it safe for them, then do so. If not, wait for help to arrive, but keep reassuring the injured person. Call 999 if the situation is a medical emergency. This is when someone is seriously ill or injured or their life is at risk.

BEAR SAYS

Stay calm. You are no help to anybody if you panic. It's OK to be scared – brave people are those who do their best even when they are scared.

Calling 999

Once you have made the decision to call the emergency services, it will help if you can tell the operator the following information:

- Your location, including the area or postcode.
- The phone number you are calling from.
- Exactly what has happened. As soon as they know where you are they will start arranging for help to come to you – they may ask for some extra information (this does not delay the ambulance).

Make sure you note down:

- The patient's age, gender (male or female), and any medical history.
- Whether the patient is conscious, breathing, and if there is any serious bleeding or chest pain.
- Details of the injury and how it happened. This will help the operator to give you important first aid advice while the emergency staff are on their way.
- If you are in the street, stay with the patient until help arrives.
- Call back if the patient's condition changes or if your location changes.
- If you are calling from a building, ask someone to open the doors and signal where the ambulance staff are needed.
- Lock away any pets or animals if possible.
- If you can, write down the patient's doctor details and collect any medication that they are taking.
- Tell the paramedics when they arrive if the patient has any allergies.

CUTS AND BRUISES

The most common injuries on any trip are cuts and bruises. These can be quite minor and can be treated using supplies from a standard first aid kit. More serious cuts and bruises may need medical attention.

Hand washing

Before dealing with any first aid situation, make sure you have washed your hands if there is time and clean water available, and wear gloves to prevent contact with any bodily fluids such as blood, vomit, urine, etc.

Cuts

1. Wash and dry your hands and wear sterile gloves if possible. Talk to the injured person, tell them what you are doing, and reassure them as you stop the bleeding. Press on the area with a clean, dry, and absorbant material for a few minutes. If something is embedded in the cut, leave it there until you have got some medical advice. You might need to press either side of it.

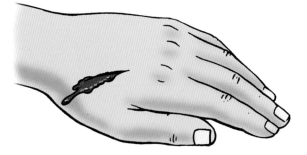

2. If the cut is on a hand or arm, raise it above the patient's head as this helps to reduce the flow of blood. If the leg is affected, get them to lie down and raise the leg above the level of the heart – you could put their foot on a chair.

3. When the cut has stopped bleeding, prevent infection by cleaning and drying it and covering it with a dressing. This may be as simple as washing the cut under the tap and popping on a plaster, or it may need cleaned with an alcohol-free wipe and covered with a sterile pad with a bandage on top. You can secure the bandage with a safety pin or sticky tape.

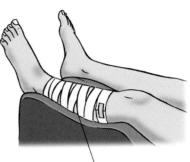

elevated leg

black eye

Bruises

A bruise is a bleed that happens under the skin when tiny blood vessels are damaged – usually as a result of a collision. Sometimes a bump also appears – this is just fluid gathering under the skin. As bruises heal, they usually change colour. A black eye is a bruise to the eye area.

1. Hold an ice pack on the bruise as soon as it happens for up to 10 minutes. A bag of frozen peas in a tea towel will work if you don't have an ice pack. If you don't have anything frozen, a clean, damp cloth is better than nothing. If the bruise is extremely swollen, painful, or doesn't go away on its own, medical advice is needed.

2. Someone who has a black eye always needs to be checked by someone with medical expertise, as it is often caused by a bump to the head.

Broken arm or wrist

If you think someone has broken their arm or wrist, look out for the following symptoms:

- Severe pain. They may not want you to touch their arm.
- Their arm may be in a strange position.
- A snap noise at the time of injury.
- Bruising and swelling.
- Tingling or numbness.
- Difficulty moving their arm.
- In the case of a very serious break, the bone may poke through the skin.

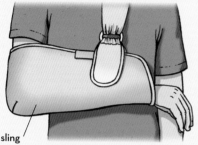

sling

How to identify a break

It is difficult to tell the difference between a sprain and a minor break. Always treat the injury as a fracture until the person has been checked by a medical professional. The patient may also feel dizzy and sick because of the shock.

Action

- If it's a bad break call for an ambulance. Otherwise, go to the nearest accident and emergency department.
- Make a sling that goes around the neck and under the arm. Keep the arm as still as possible.
- Stop any bleeding by pressing on the wound with a clean pad.
- Press an ice pack on the injured area.
- Don't let the patient eat or drink in case they need an operation to fix the broken bone.
- Stay with the injured person. Ideally, one adult will drive and another person will sit next to them in the car.

If someone breaks a limb and their bones are out of place, do not try to straighten them. Call for an ambulance. Broken legs are treated in a similar way to broken arms. Always call for medical assistance.

Sprains and strains

A sprain is the name for an injury to a ligament or tendon. It might have been stretched, twisted, or torn. Ligaments are found in the joints so the injury might be to a knee, ankle, wrist, or even a thumb.

Strains occur in the muscles and are common in the legs and back. Treatment for sprains and strains is similar.

BEAR SAYS

Usually it is recommended that you move a sprained joint again as soon as it is possible, but a muscle strain may need to be kept still for a few days.

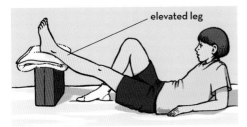
elevated leg

crutches

PRICE stands for...

Protection – use a bandage or support to stop further injury.
Rest – rest the affected joint or muscle. Ask your doctor when you can start moving it again.
Ice – wrap a damp tea towel around some ice and put in on the area for around 15 minutes every two hours for a couple of days. Don't let the ice touch your skin and don't sleep with the ice in place.
Compression – use an elasticated tubular bandage to stop the swelling, but make sure it isn't too tight as you don't want to stop the blood flowing. Take the bandage off when you go to bed.
Elevation – keep the limb raised as much as possible.

cold compress

Avoid **HARM** for three days following a sprain or strain:
Heat – don't have a hot bath or go in a sauna.
Alcohol – if alcohol is consumed the swelling may increase.
Running – don't do any exercise.
Massage – this may slow down the healing.

BITES AND STINGS

Most people who get stung will get better in a few hours or days. However, always treat bites and stings with caution as some people can have a bad allergic reaction.

Survival tips
- Never disturb bees, wasps, or hornets.
- Don't wear perfume, bright colours, or eat and drink sugary foods if you are in an area with lots of bees, wasps, or hornets.
- Don't swat them or wave your arms around – stand still.
- Wear shoes and avoid loose clothing.
- Keep vehicle windows closed.
- If the sting is left in your skin, scrape it out with a bank card or similar using a sideways motion.
- Wash the area, elevate, and apply a cold compress.
- Painkillers may help. Avoid home remedies.
- Get medical help if you vomit, feel unwell, have been stung on the mouth, throat or near the eyes, or if there is any swelling or breathing difficulties.

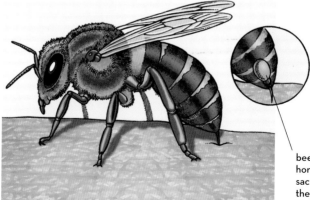

bees, wasps, and hornets have a little sac of venom that they will inject using their stinger

Jellyfish sting survival guide
- Most jellyfish stings are mild and require simple treatment.
- First, get the person out of the water.
- Remove any remaining tentacles using tweezers and wear gloves if possible.
- Apply a heat pack or put the affected area in hot water.
- Painkillers may help.
- If they have difficulty breathing, or have been stung in the face or the genitals, call for medical help.
- Vinegar has been shown to stop the box jellyfish from continuing to discharge its stingers. Despite common myths, urinating on the sting is unlikely to help.

BEAR SAYS

Always tell an adult if you've been stung, as some people can have a life threatening allergic reaction.

use vinegar on
a jellyfish sting

DROWNING

If someone is at risk of drowning, you need to stay calm and act quickly. Get them out of the water before you try to perform first aid. Never put yourself in danger to try and help someone in the water.

Survival guide

Do not put yourself in danger. If the person does not respond to you, do the following:

- Get someone else to call for an ambulance.
- Check their airway and look for signs of breathing.
- If they are breathing but unconscious put them in the recovery position (p.18–19).
- If they are not breathing, give CPR and rescue breaths (p.21).
- Keep going until they respond to you or help arrives.
- If they start breathing, keep them warm, put them in the recovery postion with their head lower than their body, keep checking their breathing and pulse, and make sure they keep talking to you until help arrives.

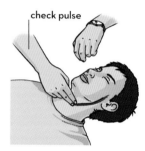
check pulse

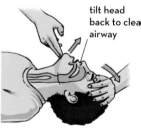
tilt head back to clear airway

BEAR SAYS

Rescue breaths and CPR are best learnt by going on a first aid course and refreshing your knowledge every year, as techniques sometimes change.

FALLS

Falls are extremely common, particularly with toddlers and older people at home. Even just falling over from standing can cause a fatal injury, so care is essential even if the fall does not appear serious. It is always worth estimating how far a person has fallen as this can help the emergency services.

Minor trips

If the person has no obvious injuries and can get up, help them to slowly move onto a chair. If you are worried or they have bumped their head, call for medical assistance. Some symptoms may appear in the hours and days after a fall, so don't leave them alone and always get them checked by a medical professional if there are any concerns. It is important to find out why the person fell over so it can be prevented in future, or they can get medical treatment if they have condition that may come back and cause them to fall again.

paramedics treating a victim of a major fall

Major falls
- Do not put yourself in danger.
- Be extremely careful not to move them if at all possible, as they may have a head or neck injury.
- Follow emergency first aid procedures.
- Ask someone to call the emergency services.
- If they aren't responsive or breathing, give rescue breaths and CPR.
- Try to stop any bleeding.

CPR can be performed anywhere

ELECTROCUTION

If an electric shock occurs in a building, there should be a place to switch off the mains supply (usually on a fuse board). It is always worth asking an adult to show you where this is located. They can look different to the one in the picture depending upon how old it is.

Survival guide
- Get an adult to switch off the mains.
- Don't go near the person or touch them until the mains supply is off.
- Follow Dr's ABC (p.20).

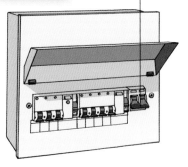

the red switches on a fuse box will turn it off

Lightning strike
Being struck by lightning is extremely rare. You can calculate how close a storm is by counting the time between a flash of lightning and a clap of thunder. If it is less than 30 seconds, you need to get to solid shelter. Get inside a building or a car. Avoid touching metal or anything that conducts electricity, and stay away from water. Golf clubs, trees, and umbrellas should also be avoided.

If you can't get indoors, crouch down, making yourself into a small ball with your feet together. Tuck your head in towards your chest and don't lie flat on the ground. Wait until around half an hour after the last flash of lightning before you come out of any shelter, as strikes are common after the storm has passed.

A person who has been struck by lightning may have very minor injuries, or they could be much more severely injured, including the possibility of cardiac arrest.

If the person isn't breathing, begin Dr's ABC and deal with any burns or bleeding.

BEAR SAYS
Do not touch anything electrical unless you have been shown how to use it by an adult and they have said that you may use it.

DIARRHOEA AND VOMITING

Diarrhoea usually clears up on its own in a few days if it's caused by an infection. Make the person drink small sips of water as often as possible, particularly if they are also being sick. Avoid fruit juice or fizzy drinks, as they can can make things worse. Take care to watch out for sign of dehydration, particularly in young children and elderly people.

Dehydration

Ideally, adults should have enough water, salt, and sugar. A bag of crisps and some diluted squash may help. Ginger is a home remedy that some people find helps with nausea. Women in early preganancy can suffer from sickness and may find that eating ginger biscuits helps them feel better.

ginger biscuits

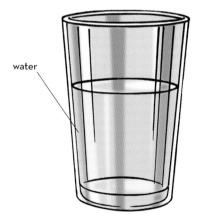

water

RECOVERY POSITION

This is used when someone is unconscious but breathing, and showing no sign of any other life threatening condition. If you suspect someone has a spine or neck injury, do not move them into the recovery position – wait for the emergency services to arrive.

Why is this helpful?

The recovery position helps to stop the patient's tongue from blocking their airway, and allows blood or vomit to drain away from their airway safely. It is the safest position to put someone in if you have to leave them.

rolling someone onto their side will help prevent their airway becoming blocked

check the airway is clear

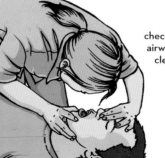

BEAR SAYS

It is useful to practise putting someone into the recovery postion. You can find video guides online to learn how to do this.

Moving someone into the recovery position

- If they are lying on the floor on their back, kneel beside them.
- Take the arm nearest to you and place it at a right angle to their body, with their hand pointing up towards their head (step 1).
- Cross the other arm over their chest and place their hand under the side of their head closest to you, with the back of their hand under their cheek (step 2).
- Bend the knee furthest away from you.
- Roll them carefully onto their side by pulling the bent knee towards you (step 3).
- Make sure their airway is open.
- Stay with them until help arrives (step 4).

Step 1
Place the arm nearest to you at a right angle, with their hand pointing up.

Step 2
Place the other hand next to their head, with the back of their hand under the opposite cheek.

Step 3
Raise the knee furthest from you and use it to pull them towards you onto their side.

Step 4
Make sure their airway is open and stay with them until help arrives.

DR'S ABC

The Dr's ABC is a good way of remembering the steps you need to take when checking a casualty.

Survival guide

talk to or shout at the person to try for a response

Danger.
You must keep yourself safe – you cannot help if you are injured too.

Response.
Ask the person their name or tell them to open their eyes to see if they are conscious. It's ok to shout.

Shout for help.
Get someone else to call the emergency services while you carry out the first aid.

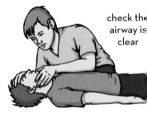

check the airway is clear

Airway.
Make sure their airway isn't blocked and is open. If they are unconscious, tilt their head back and lift their chin.

Breathing.
Look, listen, and feel for signs of breathing for 10 seconds. If the person is unconscious but breathing normally, they should be placed in the recovery position. If the casualty is unconscious and not breathing, call for an ambulance and start CPR.

check for signs of breathing

Circulation.
Check for a pulse on their wrist or the side of their neck for 10 seconds. Look for signs of bleeding – don't worry about minor cuts. Press down on any bad cuts with a clean pad and raise them above the heart if possible. Keep watching the injured person and look out for signs of shock.

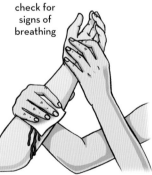

apply pressure to any cuts

CPR

CPR (Cardio Pulmonary Resuscitation) is carried out when somebody falls unconscious and stops breathing completely, or if their breathing is not normal.

Why is it important?

It is important to carry out CPR in order to help prevent brain damage. It is unlikely to restart someone's heart, but it will give the patient a better chance of recovery if the heart can be restarted with a defilbrillator.

If you are in a situation where CPR is needed, you will get help over the telephone when you call for an ambulance while the emergency services are arriving. If you are confident you can carry out CPR with rescue breaths, but otherwise you can just do hands-only CPR which is also known as chest compressions.

BEAR SAYS

CPR is really hard work and gets tiring fast. It is best if several people can take turns so that the CPR doesn't stop.

Hands only

1. Put the heel of your hand on the breastbone at the centre of the patient's chest. Person with breastbone labelled Put your other hand on top and lock your fingers together.
2. Make sure your shoulders are above your arms.
3. Use your body weight to press straight down on their chest by about 5 cm.
4. Keep your hands on their chest but relieve the pressure, allowing your hands to come back to their original position.
5. Repeat this about twice per second until the ambulance arrives.

sternum
(breastbone)

Rescue breaths

For an adult:

- Give two rescue breaths after 30 chest compressions.

- Tilt the head and lift the chin. Seal your mouth over their mouth and blow steadily and firmly into their mouth for about a second. Make sure their chest rises. Do this twice.

- Continue this cycle of rescue breaths and chest compressions until they recover or emergency help arrives.

BEAR SAYS

I cannot stress enough the value of going on a first aid course to learn this, or making sure you are supervised by an adult with first aid training.

The instructions are slightly different for children, and different again for infants under one year old. You can learn this in specialised first aid courses.

SHOCK

Shock is a life threatening condition that happens when the body experiences less blood flow than it should. It is a competely different thing to an emotional shock.

Symptoms of shock

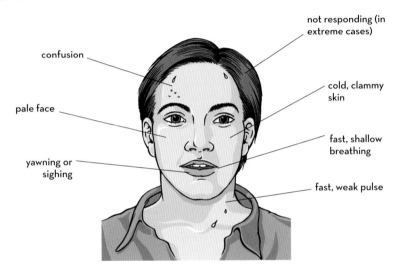

confusion

not responding (in extreme cases)

pale face

cold, clammy skin

yawning or sighing

fast, shallow breathing

fast, weak pulse

Treatment
- Lie them down with their legs raised if possible.
- Call for an ambulance.
- Loosen any tight clothing.
- Keep them warm and calm.
- Keep checking their breathing, pulse, and level of response.
- If they become unresponsive, move onto Dr's ABC.

ALLERGIC REACTIONS

Always ask people you are travelling with if they are allergic to anything. Make sure they have enough medication for the trip, and that everyone knows where it is and how to deal with any problems.

Food allergies

Nuts, fruit, shellfish, eggs, and cows' milk are commonly associated with food allergies. Allergic reactions can be life threatening but are often mild. A food allergy could cause an itchy mouth, throat, or ears, swelling, a rash, or vomiting. Anaphylaxis is life threatening and the symptoms are swelling of the mouth, difficulty breathing, light headedness, and loss of consciousness. Some people with food allergies have an auto-injector pen (EpiPen®) that contains a hormone called adrenaline that can be used in emergencies.

Food allergies

- A person with a food allergy should try and prevent a reaction by avoiding any food they know they are allergic to.
- Call for an adult and/or medical help even if the symptoms are mild or have stopped.
- Dial 999 and explain that you think someone is having a severe allergic reaction and tell the operator what you think has caused it.
- If the person has medication such as an auto-injector adrenaline pen (EpiPen®) help them to use it.
- Place them into a comfortable sitting position, leaning slightly forward to help their breathing.
- If they become unresponsive, open their airway and check their breathing.
- If they aren't breathing, CPR will need to be performed until medical help arrives.

peanuts

auto-injector pen

SPLINTERS

A splinter is when a small fragment of something, normally wood, gets stuck under your skin. It is normally quite a minor injury, but can become infected if not treated properly.

Small splinters

Make sure you have clean hands, then clean the wound with water. If it doesn't hurt, the splinter will work its own way out if it is left alone. If it hurts, you can gently touch the area with sticky tape and see if that pulls it out.

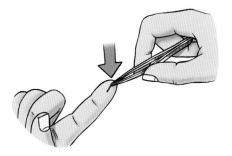

Larger splinters

Clean some tweezers with alcohol. If you can see the end of the splinter, grip it with the tweezers and pull it out in a straight line. Squeeze the wound to make it bleed slightly as this will help remove dirt. Wash and dry the wound and pop a dressing on if it is needed.

BURNS, HEATSTROKE, DEHYDRATION, AND SUNBURN

Burns can be very serious, and must be treated as soon as possible. The effects of the sun can also be serious, and it is important to take precautions when outside for long periods of time to avoid heatstroke or sunburn.

Burns

1. Keep yourself safe.
2. Stop the burning by removing the person from the area, putting water on the flames, or smothering the flames with a blanket.
3. Remove any clothing or jewellery that is close to the burnt area, but don't try to take off anything that is stuck to the skin.
4. Run the burn under lukewarm or cool water. Never use ice or any greasy substances.
5. Keep the person warm.
6. Cover the burn with cling film or a clear plastic bag.
7. Get an adult to provide a suitable painkiller.
8. Sit them upright if the face or eyes are burnt.

lukewarm
water

cover a burn
with clingfilm

BEAR SAYS

Even minor burns should be checked by a doctor or nurse, especially if the patient is under five or over 60.

Heatstroke and heat exhaustion

Heatstroke is very serious, but not as common as heat exhaustion. It occurs when a person's temperature becomes very high and their body cannot lower it without help. It can be fatal, so if you think someone may have heatstroke you need to call an ambulance. Heat exhaustion occurs when a person becomes too hot and starts to lose water or salt. They may develop heatstroke if they don't get treatment fast enough. The symptoms of heat exhaustion include tiredness and weakness, dizziness, low blood pressure, headaches, sickness, muscle cramps, heavy sweating, and extreme thirst.

Treatment for heat exhaustion

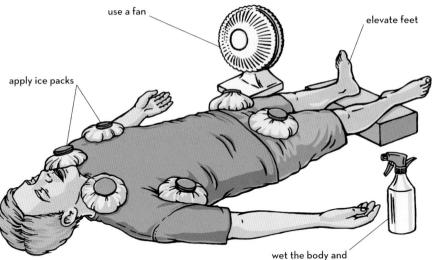

use a fan

elevate feet

apply ice packs

wet the body and
clothes - use a spray
bottle of water

Treatment

Someone with heat exhaustion needs to lie down in the shade. Remove as much clothing as possible, cool their skin with water (you could wrap them in a wet sheet), fan their wet skin, and give them plenty of water, diluted squash, or a sports drink. If they don't start to get better within 30 minutes call for medical help.

Dehydration

Dehydration happens when someone loses more fluid through sweating, vomiting, diarrhoea, or urinating than they can take in from drinking. It is important for everyone to drink plenty of water, but especially if they are exercising more than normal, are in a hot place, have a fever, have diarrhoea or vomiting, or are elderly or very young.

Treatment

Drink plenty of water, take a suitable oral rehydration solution (you can buy this in sachets from a chemist), rest, and massage cramped muscles. If the person doesn't get better fast, get them to a doctor.

oral rehydration solution

Recipe for homemade rehydration solution

You will need: 1 litre of clean water, 6 level teaspoons of sugar, ½ level teaspoon of salt.

1. Add sugar and salt to the water.
2. Be careful not to add too much sugar, which can made diarrhoea worse, or too much salt, which is harmful for children. If in doubt, add some extra water.

BEAR SAYS

Sunburn is usually preventable by making sure you stay out of the sun, cover up, and wear sunscreen. Planning is key.

Sunburn

If a person shows any signs of sunburn, move them to the shade, or preferably indoors. They should take a cool bath or shower, and then apply aftersun lotion. Ask an adult to give them a suitable painkiller if they need it. They need to drink plenty of water, and keep an eye out for signs of heat exhaustion or heatstroke.

hat
sunglasses
UV clothing
sunscreen

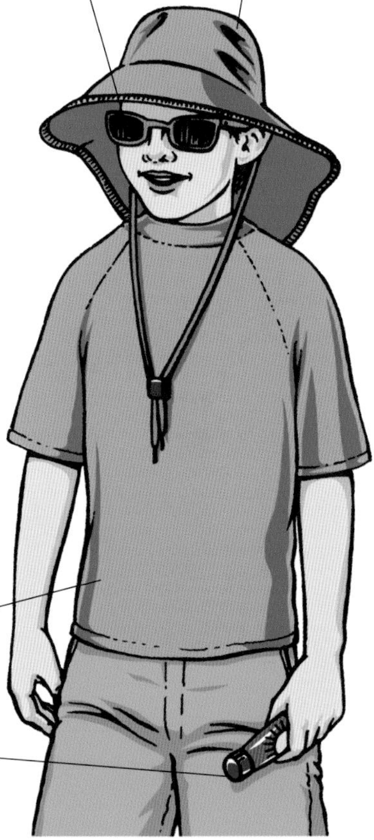

CHOKING

Choking occurs when an object, often food, gets stuck in someone's throat, making it difficult to breathe. Choking can be very serious and must be treated as soon as possible.

BEAR SAYS

It is really important not to give abdominal thrusts to pregnant women, or babies under the age of one.

Mild choking

For adults and children over the age of one, encourage them to keep coughing. Then tell them to spit out whatever is causing the problem. Don't put your fingers in their mouth.

Treatment for children under one is different, and it is best to go on a first aid course with an expert to learn how to respond to this situation.

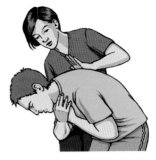

Severe choking

This is when the person cannot speak, cry, cough, or breathe. This information is for dealing with adults who aren't pregnant or children over the age of one. More care needs to be taken with younger children.

- Stand behind the person and slightly to one side. Use one hand to support their chest. Lean the person forward.
- Give up to five sharp blows between the person's shoulder blades with the heel of your hand.
- Check if the blockage has cleared.
- If not, give up to five abdominal thrusts – also called Heimlich manouvre (see below).
- If the person's airway is still blocked after trying back blows and abdominal thrusts, call 999 and ask for an ambulance.
- Continue with the cycles of five back blows and five abdominal thrusts until help arrives.
- If the person becomes unconscious and isn't breathing carry out CPR.

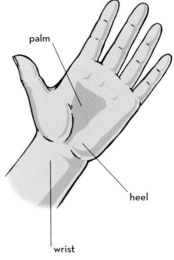

palm

heel

wrist

Heimlich manouvre

EYE INJURIES

Any injuries to the eye must be taken very seriously and treated with caution, otherwise you may risk permanent damage to the eye and loss of sight. Even a minor injury should be checked by a doctor or nurse.

Eye wound
- Lie them down and hold their head steady.
- Tell them to keep both eyes still – either look at a fixed point or close them.
- Place a clean pad over the injured eye, then use a bandage to hold it in place.
- Get medical advice.

eye washing

Small foreign body in eye
- Avoid rubbing the eye.
- Sit them down facing a light.
- Make sure your hands are clean, then gently open their eyelids with your thumbs and get them to look left, right, up, and down.
- If you can see something, ask them to blink a couple of times to see if that dislodges it (but don't keep blinking for too long, as it may scratch the eye).
- If it still hasn't gone, wash it out with clean water – pour it over the inner corner of the eye (the side nearest their nose).
- If the foreign body doesn't wash out, or it still hurts, get medical advice.

clean pad

Chemicals in eye
- Flush the eye with large amounts of water, and keep going until medical help arrives if necessary. This depends upon the chemical, but if in doubt, keep going.
- Call for medical assistance and tell the operator what the chemical was if possible.
- Keep the patient warm and reassure them – eye flushing can be uncomfortable.

BEAR SAYS
Do not attempt to remove a large foreign body from the eye. Don't press on it – call for medical help.

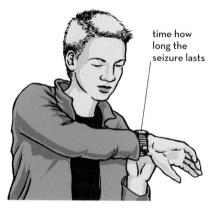
SEIZURES

Seizures can take several forms – a person may go stiff, lose consciousness, fall to the floor, and jerk about. They may just appear to be daydreaming. There are lots of behaviours that could be a type of seizure, and some are more major than others. They might lose control of their bladder or bowels, or they might bite their tongue or the inside of their mouth.

Treatment

- Protect them from injury. If possible, move furniture and harmful objects away, but don't move the patient unless they are in danger.
- Cushion their head, but don't hold them down. Don't put anything in their mouth.
- Many people with epilepsy wear jewellery or carry a card that will tell you what to do.
- Time how long the seizure lasts.
- Put them in the recovery position once any jerking has stopped.
- Keep them calm, and don't let them eat or drink until they have fully recovered.
- Call for an ambulance if you know it is their first seizure, if it lasts longer than five minutes, if they are injured, or if you feel they need medical help.

time how long the seizure lasts

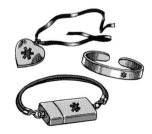

epilepsy jewellery

EMERGENCY MEDICINES FROM NATURE

It's always a good idea to carry a basic first aid kit even on very short trips, but sometimes a medical situation occurs when you have nothing to hand. Nature can sometimes provide a temporary remedy, but should be used with extreme caution as there is a risk of making things worse.

Sphagnum moss - bleeding

Sphagnum moss was collected and cleaned on a large scale to be used as a dressing for wounds during World War I. It can absorb 20 times its own volume in blood, and helps prevent infection (as long as it is clean in the first place).

sphagnum moss

Aloe vera - minor burns

After the burn has been cooled and cleaned, the sap from an aloe vera plant can be used to soothe pain and help the skin heal. It cannot be used on anything other than a very minor burn or sunburn, and all burns should still be checked by a medical professional. You can also buy aloe vera in a tube.

aloe vera

Sweet basil – insect repellent

Early Greeks and Romans thought basil would only grow if you shouted and cursed while you planted the seeds. It was used as a remedy for snakebites and scorpion stings. It is thought to repel insects, and some people keep it in their wardrobes to keep moths away from their clothes.

BEAR SAYS

You need to be absolutely sure you know what you are doing with plants. If you step out of the house pop a small first aid kit in your pocket – it makes all the difference.

basil

Making a stretcher

You need: a blanket, two long poles, and a reel of duct tape.

1. Lay the blanket flat on the floor.
2. Place the first pole in the middle of the blanket and fold the blanket over.
3. Place the second pole on top of the blanket, about 60 cm away from the first pole.
4. Fold the blanket over the poles, making sure it overlaps. Bigger blankets work better because there will be more overlap.
5. Wind the duct tape around to keep everything secure (carefully made stretchers can work even without the tape).
6. When lifting a person on the stretcher, raise the head end first, then the feet.
7. When lowering, put the feet end down gently first.

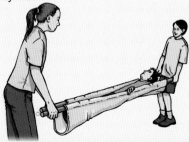

HYPOTHERMIA, FROSTBITE, AND SNOW BLINDNESS

There are many injuries and problems that can be caused by cold weather, and it's important to be aware of the best way to treat them to prevent serious injury or shock.

Snow blindness

This is a painful eye condition caused by too much exposure to the sun's rays. Symptoms may include watery or bloodshot eyes, twitching, headache, pain, and fuzzy vision. Most commonly, eyes can feel gritty.

snow goggles

Treatment

If you experience snow blindness, go inside and sit in a dark room. Keep your eyes closed, and put something over them to prevent all light from entering the eyes. Then get medical advice. Snow blindness is easy to prevent by wearing suitable sunglasses or goggles. If you have lost your goggles, you could make some by cutting slits in cardboard to limit the amount of light getting to your eyes.

Frostbite

Frostbite occurs when parts of the body freeze due to low temperatures. It is most common in fingers and toes. It can cause permanent loss of feeling in that part of the body, or the tissue can die and become gangrenous.

BEAR SAYS

Look out for symptoms of hypothermia, as a person with frostbite is likely to have hypothermia at the same time.

What to look out for

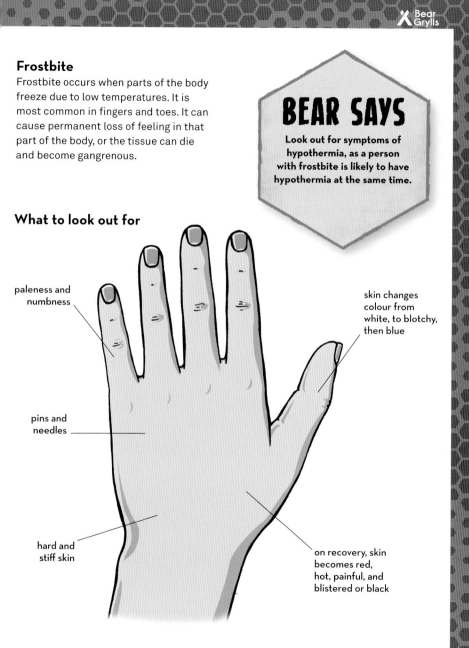

paleness and numbness

skin changes colour from white, to blotchy, then blue

pins and needles

hard and stiff skin

on recovery, skin becomes red, hot, painful, and blistered or black

BEAR SAYS

All of these cold weather conditions can be prevented by taking and wearing the correct equipment. Make sure you always follow the advice of an expert and don't take risks.

First aid

- Get them to put their hands in their armpits.
- Move somewhere warm.
- Don't rub the affected area.
- Place the affected area in warm but not hot water (about 40°C).
- Dry the area carefully and apply a light dressing.
- Raise the area above their heart to keep swelling to a minimum.
- Ask an adult to give them some suitable painkillers.
- Get them to a hospital or call for medical help.

Hypothermia

This occurs when the body temperature drops below 35°C, and is a very serious medical condition.

gns of hypothermia

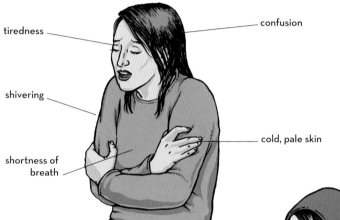

tiredness

confusion

shivering

cold, pale skin

shortness of breath

Treatment

- Move the person indoors or somewhere warm.
- Remove any wet clothing and dry the person.
- Wrap them in blankets, towels, or coats.
- Call 999.
- If they are unconscious or stop breathing, perform CPR.

HEAD AND NECK INJURIES

All head injuries should be treated as serious, as the brain is easily damaged. You should also assume that someone with a head injury also has a neck (spine) injury.

Things to look out for

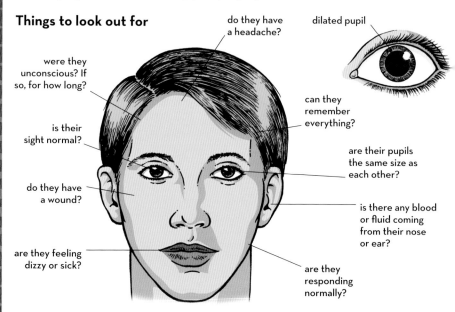

do they have a headache?

dilated pupil

were they unconscious? If so, for how long?

is their sight normal?

can they remember everything?

do they have a wound?

are their pupils the same size as each other?

is there any blood or fluid coming from their nose or ear?

are they feeling dizzy or sick?

are they responding normally?

First aid
- Sit down.
- Hold something cold on the injury.
- Treat any wounds by pressing to stop the bleeding.
- Perform DR's ABC, CPR, and rescue breaths if needed.
- Call for medical help – all head injuries need to be checked, even if they don't appear serious.

Neck injury

A person with a neck injury might
have numbness, weakness, pain,
or tingling in their arms or legs.
They may have a sore neck, back,
or head. Their neck or back may
be at a strange angle, and they
may also have a head injury.

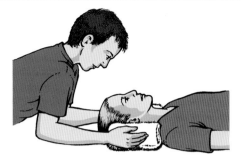

First aid

- Keep them calm and make sure they don't move.
- Kneel behind their head, rest your elbows on something to keep your arms
  steady, and grip either side of their head. Keep their head, neck, and spine in a
  straight line, but don't cover their ears.
- Keep this support until the emergency services arrive.
- You could use rolled up towels either side of their head if there is someone who
  can help you.

Log roll

A log roll is a technique that
is sometimes carried out by
several people on someone with
a spinal injury to prevent them
from choking if they are sick. It
should only be done if absolutely
necessary and you need to be
trained before attempting it.

BEAR SAYS

Be very careful not to move
a person with a neck or spine
injury, as this can cause
paralysis.

POISONING AND INTOXICATION

Poisons can occur in nature, but can also come from different chemicals you may find in your house. If you think someone has swallowed a poisonous substance, get medical help immediately.

First aid

- Get them to sit still and stay with them.
- Get them to spit out anything still in their mouth.
- Take off contaminated clothing and wash their skin with water, taking care not to get the poison on you.
- If they are unconscious, try and wake them up to spit.
- If you can't wake them up, put them in the recovery position.
- Wipe any vomit from their mouth, and keep their head pointing down.
- Don't let them eat or drink anything, don't put your hand in their mouth, and don't make them sick.
- Perform DR's ABC, CPR, and rescue breaths if needed.
- Tell the emergency services as much as you can. For example, what they swallowed, when they swallowed it, how much they swallowed, and whether it was an accident or on purpose.

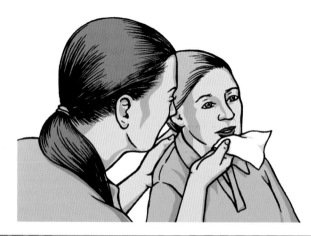

Alcohol poisoning

If someone has drunk too much alcohol, stay with them, as they are more likely to have an accident or injury because their thinking is impaired. If they lose consciousness or are being sick, get medical help, as they may be suffering from alcohol poisoning.

First aid

- Keep them sitting up and awake, and stay with them.
- Give them some water and help them drink in small sips.
- Put them in the recovery position if they are unconscious.
- Keep them warm.
- Always get an adult to help, as intoxicated people can be unpredictable and sometimes violent.
- Don't give them coffee or put them in a cold shower. Keep them still.
- If you are worried, call for medical help.

HEART ATTACKS AND STROKES

A heart attack is a medical emergency that happens when the blood supply to the heart muscle is suddenly blocked. Call for an ambulance immediately, as a heart attack can be fatal. A person having a heart attack may have lots of different symptoms, including a sharp pain in their chest, or pain travelling out from the chest into the jaw, arms, tummy, neck, or back. Symptoms are different for everyone, so if in doubt always call for medical help.

First aid

- Sit them down and make them comfortable.
- Ask an adult to decide if they should slowly chew a 300 mg aspirin tablet (children shouldn't take aspirin, and some people are allergic to it, so be careful).
- Some people have a condition called angina, and they may have a spray or tablets for this. Get it for them and give it to them if they ask.
- Check their breathing until help arrives.
- Perform DR's ABC, CPR, and rescue breaths if needed.

aspirin

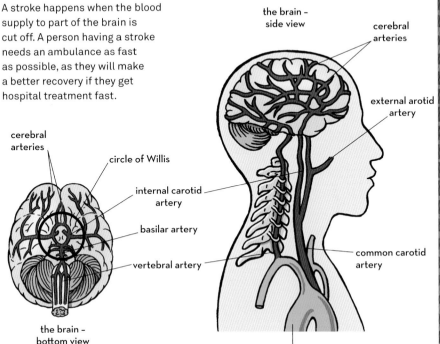

Stroke

A stroke happens when the blood supply to part of the brain is cut off. A person having a stroke needs an ambulance as fast as possible, as they will make a better recovery if they get hospital treatment fast.

Signs of a stroke

1. Face: Look at their face – is it lopsided? Can they smile? Has one eye or one side of their mouth dropped?
2. Arms: Can they lift both of their arms and keep them up? Is one weaker than the other?
3. Speech: Can they talk normally? Is their speech garbled or slurred? Can they talk at all?
4. Time: It is time to call an ambulance if you notice any of these symptoms. Tell the operator that you suspect the person is having a stroke.

BEAR SAYS

We can reduce our risk of having a heart attack or stroke by eating healthily and getting plenty of exercise.

GLOSSARY

Abdominal – around the tummy area.

Angina – chest pain that happens when the blood supply to the muscles of the heart is lower than it should be.

Cardiac arrest – when the heart stops pumping blood around the body.

Conscious – a conscious person is awake and responding to their surroundings.

Contaminated – making something unclean by contact with a poison or other unwanted substance.

Defibrillator – a machine that can give a high energy electric shock to somebody to try and restart their heart.

Dehydration – a condition that is caused by the body losing more fluid than it can take in.

Epilepsy – a condition that affects the brain and can cause seizures.

Exposure – having no protection from something harmful.

Gangrenous – a part of the body is gangrenous if it is dying because doesn't have enough blood travelling to it. Often turns black.

Ligament – connective tissue that connects a bone to another bone, often found in a joint.

Muscle – soft tissue that contracts (pulls) and relaxes to help us move our bones.

Nausea – feeling sick.

Poisonous – something that causes sickness or death by touching or entering the body.

Seizure – a sudden attack, spasm, or convulsion (used to be known as a fit).

Sterile – free from bacteria and other living micro-organisms (totally clean).

Symptoms – a physical or mental feature that gives doctors a clue that you might have a particular disease.

Tendon – tissue that connects muscles to bones.

Unconscious – an unconscious person is not awake and responding to their environment.

Urine – yellow fluid stored in the bladder (also known as wee).

Vomit – being sick.

Discover more amazing books in the Bear Grylls series:

Perfect for young adventurers, the
Survival Skills series accompanies an
exciting range of colouring and activity
books. Curious kids can also learn
tips and tricks for almost any extreme
situation in *Survival Camp*, and explore
Earth in *Extreme Planet.*

Conceived by Weldon Owen, an imprint of Kings Road Publishing,
in partnership with Bear Grylls Ventures

Produced by Weldon Owen, an imprint of Kings Road Publishing
Suite 3.08 The Plaza, 535 Kings Road,
London SW10 0SZ, UK

Copyright © 2017 Weldon Owen, an imprint of Kings Road Publishing

WELDON OWEN, AN IMPRINT OF KINGS ROAD PUBLISHING
Publisher Donna Gregory
Designer Shahid Mahmood
Editorial Susie Rae, Claire Philip, Lydia Halliday
Contributor Anne Farthing
Illustrator Julian Baker

Cover photograph copyright © by Ben Simms 2017

Disclaimer
Weldon Owen and Bear Grylls take pride in doing our best to get the facts right in putting together
the information in this book, but occasionally something slips past our beady eyes. Therefore we
make no warranties about the accuracy or completeness of the information in the book and to the
maximum extent permitted, we disclaim all liability. Wherever possible, we will endeavour to correct
any errors of fact at reprint.

Kids – if you want to try any of the activities in this book, please ask your parents first! Parents – all
outdoor activities carry some degree of risk and we recommend that anyone participating in these
activities be aware of the risks involved and seek professional instruction and guidance. None of the
health/medical information in this book is intended as a substitute for professional medical advice;
always seek the advice of a qualified practitioner.

A WELDON OWEN PRODUCTION. AN IMPRINT OF KINGS ROAD PUBLISHING
PART OF THE BONNIER PUBLISHING GROUP.